ELEMENTARY TRUTHS OF GOD'S WORD

SIX FOUNDATIONS FOR UNSHAKABLE FAITH

PASTOR TL ROGERS

T L ROGERS

Published by Mpaebo Media a division of Mike Prah, LLC, Severn, MD

U. S. LIBRARY OF CONGRESS CATALOGING-IN-PUBLICATION DATA

Rogers, Thomas Lee, Author.

Elementary truths of God's word : six foundations for unshakable faith / Thomas Lee Rogers

Mitchellville, Maryland : Mpaebo Media, 2026 | Includes Scripture references

ISBN: 978-1-969340-06-2 (paperback) | 978-1-969340-07-9 (ebook)

LCSH: Christian life—Biblical teaching | Christian doctrine—Biblical teaching | Discipleship (Christianity) | LCC: BT77 .R64 2026 | DDC 230—dc23 | LCN Case#: 1-15117048981

Printed in the United States of America. Available through major U.S. and international online book retailers. Signed copies and direct purchases are also available from the author.

CONTENTS

DEDICATION

This booklet is dedicated to Campbell McAlpine, who wrote on this subject when no one else was writing on the subject. It is from his foundational work "First Principles" that this study has been written. What you hold in your hands is an edited and revised version of that original work.

Special thanks to Stuart McAlpine for sharing his father's work with me, making it possible for this teaching to continue to bless and strengthen the Body of Christ.

FOREWORD

This book is a template outlining the basics of these six truths. If you or your pastor holds a different view on any of them, you are free to present that view.

Depending on your denomination or background, you may understand some of these truths differently. That is fine. Just make sure that everyone knows the **Basic Six Truths**.

Introduction

The Elementary Truths of God's Word — The Basics

"We have much to say about this, but it is hard to make it clear to you because you no longer try to understand. 12 In fact, though by this time you ought to be teachers, you need someone to teach you the elementary truths of God's word all over again. You need milk, not solid food! 13 Anyone who lives on milk, being still an infant, is not acquainted with the teaching about righteousness. 14 But solid food is for the mature, who by constant use have trained themselves to distinguish good from evil." (Hebrews 5:11-14, NIV)

On October 19, 1968, at 1 o'clock in the afternoon, Mable Perrin and I stood before Pastor John Meares. These are the wedding vows we said. Our marriage was built upon these six vows that are forever engraved in our minds:

1. Do you promise to love and cherish her?

2. For better or worse?

3. For richer or poorer?

4. In sickness and in health?

5. And keep her unto you?

6. So long as you both shall live?

These vows have sustained us through rocky times. Even though we did not receive premarital counseling from Bishop Meares—which is a fairly new tool today—he made sure we understood the vows. They have grounded us for 57 years. These vows became the foundation upon which our marriage—and I'm sure yours—has stood the test of time.

In those early years, when we had our struggles, I remembered those vows I had made. When I was angry, disappointed, and "fed up," those six vows rang clearly in my ears. What I had promised in those vows helped our marriage endure.

Many years later, Mable and I began conducting marriage workshops. These were for couples who already knew the basic fundamentals of marriage—the wedding vows. Everything else we taught was built on those principles. The vows are the basics.

There are many couples today who have chosen not to have a traditional marriage, yet their relationships have lasted for many years. I would suggest that even if they did not repeat those vows, their relationships are still built on the same basic commitments of love and faithfulness found in those vows. No relationship lasts without those basics.

So, I ask you—do you know the basics of your salvation?

The Elementary Truths of God's Word?

It's like 1 + 1 = 2; 2 × 2 = 4; or a, e, i, o, u are your vowels; or "an" comes before a vowel; or clockwise turns to the right and counterclockwise to the left. These are simple things—but they are foundational.

The Hebrew writer is telling his readers that they once knew these truths, but had forgotten them. Because of that, they were acting like infants, living on the milk of God's Word. His concern was that they should be teachers by now, but instead, they needed to be taught the basics again. He makes it clear—they were struggling with deeper truths because they had lost hold of the basics.

And in many cases today, many churchgoers have never really learned the basics at all.

The mature believer is able to defend what they believe and explain why they believe it.

Peter said it this way:

"But in your hearts revere Christ as Lord. Always be prepared to give an answer to everyone who asks you to give the reason for the hope that you have. But do this with gentleness and respect." (1 Peter 3:15, NIV)

The Christian should be able to clearly and confidently explain their faith.

I remember taking a course in Elementary Greek in seminary. I did very well because we were learning vocabulary and the basics of the language. The next semester was Greek Grammar, and I struggled to keep up. I went to the professor and told him I was having difficulty.

He asked me how I did in English grammar.

I told him I never really learned English grammar. I was an avid reader, so I knew what sounded right—but not why it was right.

He told me that was the problem. Greek grammar assumes you already understand English grammar.

In the same way, when deeper biblical truths are taught, there is an assumption that you already understand the elementary truths of God's Word.

All biblical teaching is built on the basics—just like $1 + 1 = 2$.

And for our purpose, those basics are found in the elementary truths of God's Word.

Truth 1—Repentance from Dead Works or Acts That Lead To Death

Different translations give different nuances of the first Elementary Truth—Repentance

> *"Therefore let us leave the elementary doctrine of Christ and go on to maturity, not laying again a foundation of <u>repentance from dead works</u> ..."*
> (Hebrews 6:1, ESV)

> *"Therefore let us move beyond the elementary teachings about Christ and be taken forward to maturity, not laying again the foundation of <u>repentance from acts that lead to death</u> ..."*
> (Hebrews 6:1, NIV)

Repentance in the Life of a Believer

The repentance spoken of here is not the initial act of repentance that everyone experiences in order to receive salvation. The Hebrew writer is writing to born-again believers. Therefore, this repentance is not that first act, but a post-conversion repentance.

Repentance is not a one-time act we perform when we first believe in Christ. It is an ongoing posture of the heart. To repent means to change one's mind and turn around. In biblical terms, it is both a turning away from sin and dead works, and a turning toward the living God.

Repentance is not about shame but about restoration. It is God's gift to bring us back into alignment with His will. When we repent, we are saying, "Lord, I agree with You about what is wrong, and I choose to walk in Your way instead."

What Are Dead Works?

The writer of Hebrews uses the phrase "dead works" to describe actions that may look religious or moral but are lifeless because they are disconnected from faith in Christ. Dead works include:

- Attempts to earn salvation by good deeds

- Rituals without heart engagement

- Works done for self-glory rather than God's glory

These works are "dead" because they lack the breath of the Spirit. True repentance leads us to abandon those works and embrace a life of faith and obedience.

Campbell McAlpine interprets *dead works* this way:

The Bible speaks of three kinds of works:

1. Works of the flesh

2. Works of the devil

3. The work of God.

There is only one work that lives and lasts forever, and that is the work of God. A dead work, then, is anything a Christian does that is not initiated by God. It will not give glory to God.

Even though you have been born again, there are still sins we are prone to commit. These do not cause us to lose our salvation, but they do not help us grow. In fact, they stunt our growth and can bring forms of death into our lives:

Relationships

Health

Marriage

Finance

Life

Emotions

There are sins which I refer to as, *"The surprising sins of the saints!"* Such sins can lead to spiritual death:

Rebellion

Gluttony

Lying or deceit

Unforgiveness

The False Appearance of Maturity

In the Bible, there is a story of two men—one who built his house on the sand and the other who built his house on a rock. The storms revealed which house was built on the wrong foundation. The house built on sand crumbled and fell. But the house built on the rock stood firm.

A similar illustration helps explain this point. My friend, Bishop Timothy Warren, has a beautiful home that he remodeled several times. At one point, he wanted to change the spindles on the stairway banister. When the carpenter began the work, he discovered that the banister had not been fastened to a floor joist, but only to the floor itself. For years, they had dealt with a wobbly banister without realizing the real problem.

So many churchgoers have the appearance of spiritual maturity, yet their lives lack steadiness, strength, and substance. They live spiritually wobbly lives, marked by inconsistency and a lack of firm conviction. Over time, this instability becomes their normal way of living. When storms arise, their lives are often shaken, fractured, and in some cases, completely destroyed—because their foundation is not firmly rooted in the elementary truths of God's Word.

Application for Today

In our modern world, "dead works" can be subtle. Serving in ministry out of duty but without love. Giving generously but for recognition. Practicing spiritual disciplines without true intimacy with God.

Repentance means asking, "Lord, where am I relying on myself instead of Your grace?"

Prayer

Father, thank You for the gift of repentance that restores my heart to You. Search me and reveal any dead works or attitudes that keep me from walking fully in Your will. Teach me to turn away from anything that does not honor You and to walk in the life and freedom You have given through Christ. May my life be marked not by empty works, but by obedience, faith, and the power of Your Spirit. Through Jesus Christ, Amen.

Reflection Questions

1. What "dead works" might I be tempted to rely on for acceptance before God?

2. How has God used repentance to bring refreshing in my life?

3. What fruit of repentance do I see growing in me right now?

TRUTH 2 — FAITH TOWARD GOD

"Therefore let us move beyond the elementary teachings about Christ and be taken forward to maturity, not laying again the foundation of repentance from acts that lead to death, and of <u>faith in God</u> (or towards God), instruction about cleansing rites, the laying on of hands, the resurrection of the dead, and eternal judgment." (Hebrews 6:1-2, NIV)

What Is Faith, Biblically Speaking?

Biblical faith is not positive thinking, wishful optimism, or confidence in our own ability. Faith is a Godward posture of trust and surrender—a Spirit-enabled confidence in the character, promises, and finished work of God. Faith takes

God at His Word and stakes life on it. It looks away from self and looks to God as the source—His nature, His promises, and His Son.

The Object of Faith Matters

Faith toward God means our confidence is anchored in who God is. We do not have "faith in faith." We trust the faithful One—Father, Son, and Holy Spirit. Because He is faithful and cannot lie, faith rests. Because He is powerful, faith expects. Because He is good, faith obeys, even when the results are not immediate.

Faith Comes by Hearing—and Responding

Scripture teaches that "faith comes by hearing ... the word of Christ" (Romans 10:17). Faith grows as God speaks through His Word, by His Spirit, and through the gospel. But faith does not stop at hearing; it responds in obedience. In the Bible, believing and obeying go together. When the Lord speaks, faith says "Yes" and takes the next step.

Case Study: Abraham—Trusting a Promise

Abraham "believed God, and it was counted to him as righteousness" (Genesis 15:6). He trusted a promise he could not yet see—descendants, a land, and blessing to the nations. His faith grew even while facing the facts: his age and Sarah's barrenness (Romans 4). Faith does not deny reality; it brings reality under the authority of God's promise.

Saving Faith and Living Faith

We are saved by grace through faith—never by works (Ephesians 2:8–9). Yet the faith that saves is a living faith. It produces fruit in love and obedience. James reminds us that true faith is seen in our works—not to earn salvation, but as evidence of new life. Grace is the root; good works are the fruit.

Common Hindrances to Faith

- Unbelief fed by fear, cynicism, or disappointment

- Double-mindedness—wavering between trust and self-reliance (James 1:6–8)

- Offense at God's timing or methods (Matthew 11:6)

- Isolation from Scripture and community, which starves faith of fuel

How to Cultivate Faith Toward God

- Stay in the Word daily; let God's voice be the loudest you hear (Romans 10:17)

- Pray honestly—bring fears, ask boldly, yield fully (Mark 9:24)

- Obey promptly in small steps; obedience strengthens faith

- Walk with faith-filled people; testimony builds your expectation (Revelation 12:11)

- Remember God's faithfulness; keep a record of answered prayers

Faith in Real Life Today

Faith is very practical. It shapes how we speak, give, forgive, and endure. In family situations, faith seeks wisdom and chooses peace. In finances, faith gives and manages with integrity, trusting God as the source. In calling and ministry, faith moves when God says move—and waits when He says wait. Faith is not reckless, and it is not fearful. It is a life of trusting and responding to God.

Prayer

Father, deepen my trust in who You are. Align my heart with Your Word, steady my steps in obedience, and teach me to rest in Your faithfulness. Through Jesus Christ, Amen.

Reflection Questions

- Where have I been tempted to have "faith in faith" instead of faith in God's character?

- What specific promise from Scripture am I choosing to trust God for right now?

- Which small step of obedience is the Lord asking me to take as an expression of faith?

TRUTH 3 — DOCTRINE OF BAPTISMS

"Therefore let us move beyond the elementary teachings about Christ and be taken forward to maturity, not laying again the foundation of repentance from acts that lead to death, and of faith in God, _instruction about cleansing rites,(Or Baptisms)_ the laying on of hands, the resurrection of the dead, and eternal judgment." (Hebrews 6:2, NIV)

Why "Baptisms" (Plural)?

Hebrews refers to "baptisms" in the plural because the New Testament presents at least two: baptism in water (the believer's public identification with Christ) and baptism with the Holy Spirit (the believer's empowerment for life and witness). These are distinct in purpose, yet they work together in the life of a disciple.

Baptism in Water

Water baptism is an outward confession of an inward change. In the water, we declare our union with Christ—buried with Him and raised to walk in newness of life (Romans 6:3–4). Baptism does not save us; Christ saves us. But baptism is an act of obedience to the command of Jesus (Matthew 28:19). It is a public witness that we now belong to Him.

Baptism with the Holy Spirit

Jesus promised His followers power when the Holy Spirit came upon them (Acts 1:8). To be baptized with the Spirit is to be filled with His presence and power for bold witness, holy living, and fruitful service. The Spirit lifts up Jesus, helps us understand Scripture, convicts us of sin, gives spiritual gifts, and produces Christlike character in us. We are to live continually filled with the Spirit (Ephesians 5:18).

Living a Baptized Life

A baptized life is lived out daily. It means remembering who we are in Christ through water baptism. It means walking by the Spirit so we do not follow the desires of the flesh (Galatians 5:16). It means serving others with the gifts God has given us, in love (1 Corinthians 12–13).

Prayer

Lord Jesus, thank You for uniting me with Yourself and for the gift of the Holy Spirit. Root me in my new identity and fill me afresh for holy living and bold witness. Amen.

Reflection Questions

1. How does my water baptism shape my identity and daily witness to Christ?

2. Where do I sense the Holy Spirit inviting me to be freshly filled and obedient today?

3. What specific step can I take this week to walk by the Spirit in a practical way (Galatians 5:16)?

TRUTH 4 — LAYING ON OF HANDS

"Therefore let us move beyond the elementary teachings about Christ and be taken forward to maturity, not laying again the foundation of repentance from acts that lead to death, and of faith in God, instruction about cleansing rites, <u>the laying on of hands,</u> the resurrection of the dead, and eternal judgment." (Hebrews 6:1-2, NIV)

From Genesis to the early church, laying on of hands signifies identification, blessing, consecration, and impartation. In the Old Testament, leaders laid hands to set apart successors (Joshua) and to identify offerings. In the Gospels, Jesus touched the sick and blessed children. In Acts, the apostles laid hands when commissioning servants, praying for the sick, and in moments where believers received the Holy Spirit. Across these scenes, the act is not mechanical; it is a prayerful sign of God's gracious activity—His presence, power, and purpose at work.

Why Do We Lay Hands?

Blessing and Encouragement:

As Jesus blessed children (Mark 10:16), leaders and communities may bless with tenderness and dignity.

Healing Ministry:

Jesus "laid His hands on every one of them and healed them" (Luke 4:40). The church continues to pray for the sick, trusting God to heal according to His will.

Commissioning and Sending:

The church laid hands on servants and missionaries (Acts 6:6; 13:2–3), recognizing God's call and committing them to His grace.

Impartation for Service:

Paul references gifts connected with the laying on of hands (1 Timothy 4:14; 2 Timothy 1:6), reminding us that ministry flows from God's grace, not human striving.

The Seriousness of Spiritual Transfer

Scripture cautions, *"Do not be hasty in the laying on of hands"* (1 Timothy 5:22). The gesture is not casual. We lay hands with clean motives, sober judgment, and accountability. Leaders should be tested in character and doctrine. We do not manipulate outcomes or place confidence in the act itself; our trust is in the Lord who answers prayer.

Practicing with Wisdom and Care

Consent and Care:

Always ask permission and honor personal boundaries. Choose appropriate, non-invasive touch.

Prayerful Posture:

Depend on the Holy Spirit; keep Scripture central; exalt Jesus, not a person or gift.

Community and Accountability:

Minister in teams when possible; involve elders; provide follow-up and discipleship.

Holiness and Integrity:

"Clean hands and a pure heart" (Psalm 24:4). Guard against pride, pressure, or showmanship.

Prayer

Father, thank You for calling and equipping Your people. Teach me to minister with humility and love. Use my hands as instruments of Your blessing, healing, and commissioning—always under Your Word and led by Your Spirit. In Jesus' name, Amen.

Reflection Questions

1. In what ways is God inviting me to be a vessel of blessing, encouragement, or healing to others?

2. Where might I need to slow down, seek counsel, or strengthen character before laying hands or receiving ministry?

3. Who is the Lord highlighting for encouragement or commissioning, and how can I pray and support them this week?

TRUTH 5 — RESURRECTION OF THE DEAD

"Therefore let us move beyond the elementary teachings about Christ and be taken forward to maturity, not laying again the foundation of repentance from acts that lead to death, and of faith in God, instruction about cleansing rites, the laying on of hands, <u>the resurrection of the dead,</u> and eternal judgment." (Hebrews 6:1-2, NIV)

The Christian Hope

Resurrection is at the heart of the Christian hope. We do not hold on to vague ideas of "a better place." We believe in a real, bodily resurrection, based on the empty tomb of Jesus. Because Christ rose physically, our future is not an escape from the body, but a renewed life with Him forever (1 Corinthians 15).

Jesus, the First Fruits

Scripture calls Christ the *"first fruits"*—the first of the harvest that guarantees the rest (1 Corinthians 15:20). His resurrection is not an isolated event; it is the promise of ours. The same power that raised Jesus from the dead is now at work in us who believe (Ephesians 1:19–20). This assures us that death is defeated and that our labor in the Lord is not in vain.

What Kind of Resurrection?

The Bible teaches a real, bodily resurrection. Our future bodies will be recognizable, yet changed—imperishable, glorious, powerful, and Spirit-filled (1 Corinthians 15:42–44). There is continuity—it is truly us. And there is change—no decay, no sickness, no death. Resurrection is not reincarnation, and it is not just coming back to life as before. It is a complete renewal by the power of God.

Timing and Order—What We Know for Certain

Believers who die are *"with Christ"* (Philippians 1:23). At the Lord's return, *"the dead in Christ will rise first,"* and those who are alive will be caught up together with them (1

Thessalonians 4:16–17). God has not revealed every detail, but He has told us what we need to know: Christ will return, the dead will be raised, and His people will be with Him forever.

Living in Light of Resurrection Now

Holiness:

Because a glorious future awaits, we pursue purity today (1 John 3:2–3).

Perseverance:

Resurrection hope strengthens us in trials; *"your labor in the Lord is not in vain"* (1 Corinthians 15:58).

Comfort:

We grieve, but not as those without hope (1 Thessalonians 4:13). Our tears matter to God and will be wiped away (Revelation 21:4).

Mission:

Because death is defeated, sharing the gospel is urgent and worth our lives.

Resurrection Power for Today

The same Spirit who raised Jesus from the dead lives in us (Romans 8:11). Resurrection is not only a future promise; it is present power. God brings life to the dead places in our hearts. He restores what is broken, renews our strength, and gives hope where there was despair.

Prayer

Risen Lord, anchor my heart in Your victory over death. Fill me with resurrection hope and power today, so that I may live holy, stand strong in trials, comfort others, and serve You with joy. Amen.

Reflection Questions

1. Where do I need the Holy Spirit's resurrection power to bring new life today?

2. How does the promise of a bodily resurrection reshape my choices and priorities this week?

3. Who can I comfort or encourage with the hope of resurrection, and how will I do it?

Truth 6 — Eternal Judgment

"Therefore let us move beyond the elementary teachings about Christ and be taken forward to maturity, not laying again the foundation of repentance from acts that lead to death, and of faith in God, instruction about cleansing rites, the laying on of hands, the resurrection of the dead, <u>and eternal judgment.</u>" (Hebrews 6:1-2, NIV)

The Certainty—and Goodness—of God's Judgment

God's judgment is not the opposite of His love; it is part of His holy love. Because God is just, evil will not have the last word. At the cross, justice and mercy meet. Jesus took our judgment so that all who trust in Him can be forgiven, made right with God, and brought into His family.

Judgment, then, is both serious and full of hope—evil is dealt with, what is right is honored, and God's grace is lifted up.

Two Judgments in View

The Judgment Seat of Christ (Bēma) — for believers:

This is an evaluation of our works, not a judgment for salvation (2 Corinthians 5:10; 1 Corinthians 3:12–15). Faithful service, right motives, and obedience are rewarded. Works done for self or without sincerity will not last. The believer is saved, but some rewards may be lost.

The Great White Throne — for the unrepentant:

Revelation 20:11–15 shows the final judgment for those who reject God's grace. This reminds us that everyone is accountable to God. His judgment is right, and no wrong will go unanswered.

Rewards, Motives, and Accountability

Scripture speaks of rewards as the Lord's way of honoring faithfulness—the "well done" from Him (Matthew 25). These rewards are not something we earn, but a recognition of faithful living. Our motives matter—love, humility, and obedience. Knowing we will give an account helps us live right, even in the things no one else sees.

Living with Eternity in View

Holiness:

We live pure lives because we know we will see the Lord (1 John 3:2–3).

Reconciliation:

We forgive quickly and make things right while we have the opportunity (Matthew 5:23–24).

Mission and Mercy:

Judgment fuels urgency for evangelism and compassion for the lost (Jude 22–23). We warn with tears and invite with hope, pointing to the Savior who bore judgment in our place.

The Gospel and Assurance for Believers

For those who are in Christ, there is no condemnation (Romans 8:1). Our judgment was placed on Jesus. Our names are written in the Book of Life. The Judgment Seat of Christ does not threaten our salvation—it reminds us to be faithful. We do not live in fear, but in readiness and gratitude.

Prayer

Righteous Father, thank You that justice and mercy meet at the cross. Help me to live with eternity in mind—holy, forgiving, and compassionate—so that my life honors Jesus and blesses others. Strengthen me to hear Your "well done." In Jesus' name. Amen.

Reflection Questions

1. How does the reality of the Judgment Seat of Christ reshape my motives and priorities this week?

2. Is there someone I need to forgive or reconcile with as a step of obedience before God?

3. Who can I lovingly point warn and invite to Christ, and what is one practical step I will take?

Closing Summary

These six elementary truths form the sturdy foundation upon which a life in Christ stands:

1. Repentance from dead works

2. Faith toward God

3. Baptisms (in water and with the Holy Spirit)

4. The laying on of hands

5. The resurrection of the dead, and

6. Eternal judgment

They are not ideas to be admired from a distance, but realities to be lived—truths that shape our worship, our work, our relationships, and our hope.

Build on these, and keep building. Teach them to the next generation. Let them steady your emotions in storms, bring clarity to your decisions in times of confusion, and move you to obedience in every season. When the foundation is sure, the house can stand and grow.

We look to God alone as our source. We are always moving toward Him.